10 Steps How To Keep A Man

How Not To Run Him Off

Larry Wooten

 ISBN: 9781089018162

Table of Contents

Introduction

Do you find that dating is too confusing? You might get attention from men, but then they don't seem to hang around for too long. When the same challenges present themselves time after time, it can be easy to conclude that all men are the same and that it is probably easier to stay single, but often problems arise because we don't know the best ways to control our instincts and communicate our value and needs in relationships. And that's why many women make the dating mistakes that cause a man to lose interest early on. Do you want to know how to keep a man interested? Then read on. Because when you fully understand this advice you won't stay single for long.

If you want a strong, loving relationship, then you need to understand what really makes a man feel good. There is a certain type of woman that a man is irresistibly attracted to. She knows how to captivate him and communicate with him to draw him close and get him to respond in the ways that she wants.

Step 1

Become The Best Cook You Can Be

Ladies, I know that we are all "independent women, fancy, or a 5-star chick," but it means nothing if you can't cook. Men love food. A woman who can cook is a treasure to a man. That's just a FACT.

The old adage "The way to a man's heart is through his stomach" is 100 percent accurate. A woman that cooks also reminds him of their mother and confirms that their family present or future will be taken care of. No man wants to eat ramen noodles, boxed mac and cheese or PB&J sandwiches all the time, but instead some homemade cornbread, collard greens, candied yams and any fried meat without blood running from it. If you are a meat eater. And, you should also be able to cook a hot breakfast and not just pour cereal into a bowl.

Think about a caveman - he goes out in the land to hunt to provide his family with food. When he gets back home, he doesn't want to call the local pizza spot and order dinner because his mate can't do anything with the buffalo he just dragged back. Secondly, I know that we are all busy with our careers and that fast food is a convenience, but when you are feeding your "Boo," please don't race through the drive-through to get a burger or chicken nugget combo.

Additionally, so many times we get caught up in "Well, he should like me for who I am and if he can't handle that I don't cook, then he can kick rocks." That's all good, but you will not keep him very long, as he will leave you for someone who is not afraid to get in the kitchen to at least try to cook some real food. You don't have to be an "Iron Chef," but you need to know how to cook. If you don't know, then take some time out to learn. I'm absolutely certain that you have some old-school women in your family who prefer cooking over fast food, any day. Call Big Momma or one of your older aunties and get some recipes; grab a cookbook or do some research online. There are too many websites that provide very simple, home cooked meals. Take some time out to learn how to cook a few dishes.

Men find it very attractive and wonderful when a woman can create all the things that their stomach craves while looking good doing it. I know that the whole “woman in the kitchen” idea just perpetuates the male-dominated patriarchal culture in which we live. I’m just presenting the idea that men, given the choice, will always choose a woman who can cook over one who can’t. Ladies, please don’t shoot the messenger. I am not saying to only learn how to cook to appease a man; however, it will make you more “marketable” to a man. And, at the end of the day, you still have to eat.

Step 2

Keep Sex Ready & Willing

The importance of sex in a healthy relationship cannot be understated. Well, mostly. See, for a guy, it's definitely one of the most important things if not the most important thing. It's a primal thing, really. On the other hand, many women would say it's just as important, but may be more likely to overlook the issue if everything else in the relationship is going well.

Here's a simple way to sum things up: Men often choose a woman based upon the sex or the prospect of it, and end up falling in love; while women generally choose a man based upon the love they feel, and end up enjoying sex. I know that "all" is a total generalization, but you get my point. Men tend to focus on sex. Women tend to focus on love.

The implications of all these factors are big because sex is a deep and powerful form of intimacy. It bonds and connects two people in ways that few other things can. It's beyond the mind. It's beyond the body, too. There is a deep energetic connection that bonds two people when they make love. It's not just the intermingling of juices. It's not even that two people shared an act of love with someone that they most likely hold sacred. What's really happened is that there has been a union between two people that transcends time and space. And we know it. Yet it's very hard to quantify. Right? We all know how close we feel to someone after we have sex. That doesn't mean it's the magical elixir for all that might be off or dysfunctional in a relationship.

But, heck, it sure does mean that it helps bring us together. The term "makeup sex" is just that. It brings us closer. If you've had a hard day and your hackles are all up towards your partner, yet at the end of the day you go to bed and make love, then the chances are that you will soften towards them and feel closer after making love.

I know many women may be saying that they just can't have sex when they don't feel close to their partner. It's a valid point. I'm not saying you should. What I am suggesting is this: if you want to feel more connected to your partner but are allowing squabbles and minor disagreements set your emotional agenda, simply let this anger fall away. Consider that the simple act of saying "yes" to your partner, and to passion, may begin to shift the dynamic. If you're both honoring each other correctly, sex will most likely help you feel closer to your love.

Keep this in mind too, there are many things you can do that are flirtatious, intimate and nourishing besides just the act of sex. Foreplay is lots of fun and definitely helps set the tone for better lovemaking. It for sure creates more emotional intimacy which strengthens the bonds of lovemaking.

Step 3

Know When To Give Him Space

It has really become a common joke about the man in a relationship needing 'more space', but it surely is no joke when it actually happens. It is perfectly natural to want to spend every waking minute of your day with him, but there are times when giving him space is probably the best thing you can do.

Many women also believe that the 'space reason' is another way to escape commitment issues. While this may be right in many instances, sometimes giving your boyfriend space is the best thing that you can do for him. It is also important to realize this early, so that you don't have to wait for him to say those three dreaded words - 'I Need Space'.

If you find him acting weird sometimes, and he tries to stay alone or prefers doing his own thing rather than spending time with you, it is probably a sign that, now more than ever, you do need to give him space for his and your own happiness. Here are some suggestions to do it right.

Back to the Start - Go back to doing things you used to do before he came into your life. There must be a hobby that you used to love before it took a backseat; start doing that again. Start meeting up with your pals more often, or if you don't have many, make some new ones. Become more involved in your career, and start becoming serious about that promotion. Find a motive or purpose in life that will occupy a decent amount of your day. By investing time in yourself, you give him time to do the things he likes, and he would definitely start appreciating your presence in his life, and start missing you more and more eventually.

Friends Outside the Relationship are Essential - You two might be the best of friends, but this doesn't mean that he prefers sharing every little detail of his day with you. There are certain things that he doesn't share, because those things just don't concern you. There's no need to feel offended by this. As you have your 'Girl Talks' that can only be shared with the fairer sex, 'Guy Talks' do exist and can only be shared with guys. Encourage him to be with his friends, most guys have a designated day or activity through which they enjoy their time with their friends. Don't be the over-possessive girlfriend, and give him space to do his own thing. Also don't make him spend more time with you, doing things that he actually hates, by just making him feel guilty. Try to be a cool girlfriend, and more importantly a friend. For once, empathize with his situation. In time, he'll surely return the favor, and be more than happy to allow you to spend more time with your gal pals.

His Hobbies Matter to Him - No matter how vain and neurotic his model building, his carpentry, his collection of baseball cards, his Sunday football, or his obsession with the latest smartphones and gadgets may seem to you, they are extremely important to him. They are his hobbies and they do matter. Allow him to indulge in his passion by not passing judgment or remarks on his preferences. Many men believe that reading Cosmo and shopping for clothes, bags, and shoes is a waste of time, but you do it anyway. Neither you nor your boyfriend will ever understand these quirks, but showing that it is alright to have them is important for a long-lasting relationship. Remember, not all hobbies need to be productive, sometimes they just need to make you feel happy.

Accept His Silence - There are times when you find him awfully quiet and lost. You really want to know and help, but he prefers being that way, and gets angry if asked too much. Let him be, sometimes men don't like talking about things that bother them. They prefer being alone and dealing with issues their way. There are just two ways to go about it - he will talk or he won't. If he does then great, but if he doesn't then don't force him to. It is best for both of you to respect his privacy, he will eventually get comfortable and share things with you, but till then be patient.

Don't Get Clingy - It is a proven fact that spending time together is extremely essential for the survival of a relationship, but it is also true that spending too much time together leads to its untimely demise. Although you would want to spend every waking minute with him, he really doesn't feel the same way. You surely are an important part of his life, but his life does constitute of various other things. Manipulating him into spending more time with you can give rise to harsh feelings and make him feel confined. We all deserve a little time to ourselves and hate running on a timetable. Give him some time alone to miss and appreciate your presence in his life.

Avoid Putting a Curfew - Since you're both adults here, there is no need to put a curfew on your boyfriend's outings. Also constant calling or messaging to check up on him puts you across as a desperate, needy, and over-controlling girlfriend. Explain to him that you have no issues with his outings, and only expect to know where he is going, with whom he is going, and what time will he be back. You aren't keeping tabs on his outings, it is just for you to feel secure and relaxed. Also don't go bonkers if he sometimes comes an hour or so late. He might have a genuine reason that explains his late arrival, so hear him out before doing anything.

Relax and try to be the woman and friend he fell in love with. In addition to loving him, don't forget to love yourself, and figure out a way to do things together and apart. This will help surely cement the bond of your relationship, and help it last a lifetime.

Step 4

Be Sure To Be Cleaner

When talking to friends about their relationships, one of the biggest areas of conflict that seem to keep coming up is household chores. Specifically, the problem of a 'clean' person living with a 'messy' person and the problem of who does what around the house. You probably already know by now if you are a messy person or a clean person. This is probably especially apparent if you are living with someone of the opposite type. If you've ever gotten into a big argument with your partner about cleaning, here are some suggestions for alleviating some of that conflict.

Household chores are often a battleground for breeding miscommunication and resentment if problems are not addressed and if a plan or compromise can't be reached. In fact, according to a 2007 Pew Research Poll, cleaning and doing household chores was in the top three highest-ranking issues associated with a successful relationship - third only to faithfulness and good sex.

Since the conflict comes from varying priorities, talking through these differences is key to getting on the same page. Talk with your partner or roommate and define what is dirty, messy and clean to each of you. In this conversation, it might be helpful to describe what your ideal home is like, in regards to cleanliness. Maybe explain the reasons why it is important for you to have a clean space, i.e. "It is important for me to have a clean kitchen because it motivates me to cook more." Or "It is important for me that the bedroom is clutter-free because a clean environment helps me to relax," In a relationship, it will also be helpful to acknowledge tendencies to nag or mock, i.e. nagging to get the other person to clean, or mocking the other person for caring about cleanliness. Make a list of chores that need to get done every day, things that need to get done each week and things that need to get done each month. Allocate responsibilities accordingly.

If you need some motivation, invite friends over and resolve to clean together. This is obviously not a solution for every time, but I have found that the times when my partner and I are both on the same page about cleaning is when we know that we are going to have guests come over. Another way to motivate and get on the same page is to plan for deep-cleanings. Schedule a few hours once a month where both of you agree to spend that time cleaning. This way, both of you are agreeing to make cleaning a priority during that time. This can also serve as a great re-set button for the next few weeks of trying to instill consistent and manageable cleaning habits.

Step 5

Keep It 100

Can you really tell a man everything on your mind - even the not-so-pretty stuff? Yes, as long as you know these critical elements about how to communicate with him first.

Has a man ever told you of some plans he had to hang out with his friends, or travel somewhere by himself for whatever reason, and you pretended to be perfectly okay with it because you didn't want to seem "needy?" But then later, when he came back…BAM!

All those hurt, angry feelings came out, he withdrew, and then there's a wedge between the two of you. You might conclude that you can't be honest with a man, when in reality a little tweaking in terms of timing and delivery can make all the difference…

Here's something you may not know about men, or even agree with, but it's true. A man absolutely wants you to be honest and straightforward with him. This is what men like so much about the way they can communicate with each other. And, in fact, it drives them nuts when you aren't open and direct. If they are planning something that you don't agree with, they want you to let them know at the start – as soon as possible – before it becomes a bigger issue or concern. Here's the beauty of telling a man what you think early on: it allows you to communicate in a way that's less combative and negative than it would be if you were to have it fester in your mind for a while.

Men don't "automatically" get upset when you let them know how you feel about something. They get upset when they see that you are upset. See, for most men, when a woman tells them something that isn't great about their relationship, men take it very personally. He'll instantly feel like you are blaming him – even though you might not be. Why? Men like to think and believe that the woman they're with respects them and sees them as a great man. So when a woman shares something that isn't "perfect," a man will take it as you thinking that he is not good enough and not just that something happened in your relationship that can easily be changed or improved in the future. To stop this cycle of a man feeling criticized, or like he doesn't please you, you first need to find a "safe space" before you talk and share your feelings with him.

Create a safe space for both of you to open up. By "safe," I mean telling a man that what you think, feel, and need will not jeopardize your connection, but instead make it stronger. Here's your action plan: sit down with him today at some time when you're both settled and relaxed. Then tell him that you respect his feelings, and that you appreciate the way he respects yours. (If you don't believe this right now, simply the act of communicating these words will have a profoundly positive effect on him and actually help create more respect and appreciation – because you get what you give!) Then explain that communicating as early as possible and allowing that safe space to tell each other how you really feel and that you need to be open and honest with each other in the moment is crucial to your happiness – yours and his.

What you're doing here is essentially agreeing together to accept and allow for each other's real feelings – regardless of whether they happen to please the other person in that moment. This kind of real and authentic honesty is the first step, and the one and only path to a real, secure, and lasting relationship where both partners know that their feelings are heard and respected.

Step 6

Keep Your Ex's Away

Breaking up used to mean you said goodbye, stashed some memorabilia in a shoe box, then moved on. Technology has foiled the easy break by completely changing the game. With Facebook, email, Snapchat, Twitter, and Instagram (the list goes on), your ex is easily accessible, easy to spy on, and easy to get in touch with. It's as dangerous as it sounds. After a breakup you may find yourself scanning your ex's Facebook wall for signs of a new relationship or delving into old photos of the two of you together. Simply put, technology has made the art of breaking up a little more complicated.

Keeping tabs on your ex may seem harmless enough until a new relationship enters the scene. You may go from dinner with your current partner to shooting your ex a quick Facebook message to say hi. It may seem like a meaningless gesture, but is it? Before you get too deep into your relationship with your ex, keep in mind that what may seem like a harmless relationship has the power to ruin your current relationship or at the very least, damage it. Keep these things in mind if you just can't seem to let your ex fade out of your life.

Your ex may feel like there is a potential of you all getting back together if you still speak consistently. Even if you're happy in your current relationship, maintaining a relationship with your ex may lead them to believe that they have a chance. They may think that you want to give it another shot or are secretly unhappy or unfulfilled in your current relationship. If that's true, then you need to stop and re-evaluate your current relationship. If it's not, you need to be clear with your ex about where you stand. Be blunt and honest. Let them know that you are not only dating someone else, but that you are serious about trying to make the relationship work. While there are circumstances where your ex either has to be in your life or you have developed a completely platonic friendship, you should always set clear boundaries to let your ex know where your priorities lie.

Does your partner know how often you and your ex talk? Are they aware of how present your ex is in your daily life? If they are, and they're fine with it, you're off the hook. If they don't, take a moment to think of how they would feel if they knew the extent upon which you still communicate with and rely on a romantic relationship from your past. By choosing to maintain a relationship with your ex and not being upfront with your partner, you are hurting the person you love and in a way, prioritizing your relationship with your ex.

Be honest with yourself on your need to have your ex in your life. Does it provide a mere ego boost? Are you keeping them on the back burner should your current relationship fail? Or is there more to it? Do you genuinely care about them as a friend or are you in a situation where they're part of your daily life? If it's the latter, then you'll need to have an open conversation with your partner to determine a plan on how to move forward.

Your partner may not be giving you their all if they feel you are still attached to someone else. By keeping your ex in your life, you may be limiting the potential of your current relationship. One study cited by YourTango found that staying close with an old flame can seriously affect the foundation of an existing romantic relationship. Consider all the time and energy you put into maintaining a relationship with your ex when that time and energy should go into building your current relationship. Would your current relationship be more open, honest, and deeper? The very act of juggling two people, the past, and the present has the ability to tarnish or cheapen the relationship you're currently in.

You may have considered how your relationship with your ex could hurt your partner and your relationship, but keeping an ex on the back burner can also hurt your own emotional growth. By not letting go of the past, you're keeping yourself from moving forward to discover the love and intimacy you deserve. By keeping a connection to the past in your life, you could be causing yourself unnecessary hurt and preventing yourself from progressing emotionally.

Keep in mind that your relationship with your ex ended for a reason. They weren't able to give you what you needed, and so you made the decision to move on. You deserve better, so don't let your own insecurities and fears keep you tied to an unhealthy past.

Step 7

Understand That Men Look

You're sitting with your boyfriend (or husband) in your favorite restaurant, having a wonderful night out together, when a woman walks by your table. You watch as the man you love turns his head, looks her up and down, and his eyes linger just a little too long on her breasts, or her backside.

Suddenly there's a surge of emotion, jealousy, anger, pain, insecurity. A torrent of questions runs through your mind: Does he want her? Does he thinks she's more beautiful than me? Is he not attracted to me anymore?

Sound familiar? That's because it's probably happened to every woman, at some point. Because, let's face it, men like to look. To be clear, that's all men; not just your man, not just single men, not just players and cheaters and womanizers, but all men.

Please be careful because this is how you can turn your good man into a liar. Men want a cool lady. A partner he can be the real him around. A part of being himself is looking. You want him to be honest with you. I get it, how women can take looking as disrespect. But, a part of being himself is looking. Remember you want to keep him honest. Lying is lying. So if he is not looking, it's only because he's fighting it, and if he continues to fight it he will start sneaking a look. He can't help it. Once he starts lying to himself, watch out. He'll say to himself, "I'm not going to look. She's not my type anyway." He looks at everything when he's alone. But he's trying to be on good behavior. But, this is the type of behavior that he won't be able to sustain. Eventually, the real him will return.

And on the flip side, it's hilarious when a woman is dating a guy and a woman that she thinks, is hot comes by. Usually, you see her coming before he does. In your mind, you're thinking don't bring your pretty ass over here. But, here she comes anyway. So then you start doing what I call, "Eye Glue." You know, what eye glue is. That's when you have your best eye contact of the night. You know how the super eye contact starts when your keeping track of his eyes. Making sure he doesn't look at her. You don't want this because this is the start of the sneaky man. Trust me you would prefer straightforward borderline rude dude than a liar. A real man that is into you will know not to go overboard looking. So relax he's here with you. ENJOY

Take me for instance. I’ve been with my partner for nearly 10 years. I love and adore her. I want to spend the rest of my life with her. I wouldn’t dream of betraying her trust by sleeping with someone else. But I look. I can’t help but notice when a beautiful woman walks by smelling gooood. I can’t help but react in the way that I do, to be attracted to women with certain features. It’s in my nature. And I am not alone.

It’s completely normal for men to look at other women. It’s also completely normal for women to have that visceral, emotional reaction when they catch their partner looking. It’s completely natural to want to know why men look, and what the look means.

Allow me to explain…

What "The Look" Means

- He finds her physically attractive.
- When he saw her, a chemical reaction happened in his brain. Neurotransmitters like dopamine and serotonin were released, giving him an involuntary surge of pleasure.
- Part of him wants her, or wonders what it would be like to be with her, in a completely harmless and innocent way.

Just like you might be sexually attracted to Denzel Washington, Channing Tatum or Ghost, and wonder what that might be like but you wouldn't act on it. In an alternate universe where he was single and unattached, he might be interested in her as a sexual partner.

What It Doesn't Mean

- He finds her more beautiful than you.
- He isn't attracted to you.
- He isn't happy with you, and your relationship.
- You don't satisfy him.
- You aren't (attractive, skinny, sexy, loving, affectionate, etc.) enough for him.

- You should be angry at him, or jealous of her, or insecure about yourself or your body.
- He is unfaithful, or that he is going to cheat on you.
- Your relationship is doomed.

Simply put, him looking has nothing to do with you at all. The world is full of beautiful sights – flowers and sunsets, great works of art – none more beautiful than the female body. It doesn't take anything away from you when your man admires a painting or sculpture. It doesn't diminish his love for you when he looks at another woman.

For men, sexual attraction and emotional connection do not necessarily go hand in hand. We can be attracted to women on a strictly physical level. We can be turned on by women with whom we feel no emotional connection or compatibility. We can be head-over-heels in love, completely devoted to one woman, and still be attracted to other women. In fact, science suggests that we can't help it.

This is usually interpreted as being the result of evolution. Generally speaking, women evolved to be wives and mothers, nurturers and caretakers, while we men are programmed to ensure the survival of our genes by "sowing our seeds" as far and wide as possible. You could say that our eyes are hardwired to wander. It's not a personal choice, it's a biological instinct. And it's usually acted on before the slower, conscious decision-making process kicks in.

While it is normal for men to notice other women, to look and admire, and even fantasize a bit, there is a line of respect that a mature and committed man will not cross. Looking is one thing, staring is another; and it can be hurtful, embarrassing and offensive. As I said before, I cannot help my momentary reaction when I see an attractive woman. But once the moment passes, I quickly turn my attention back to the love of my life, the woman to whom I am faithfully devoted.

When you do notice your man looking at another woman, don't read too much into it. Remember what it means, and most importantly what it doesn't. A glance does not equal a betrayal. Remember that he loves you, he cares about you, he is committed to you, and he is still attracted to you. Of all the women in his life, he chooses to be with you.

We all need love and emotional connection in order to be happy and fulfilled; men are no exception. Many cultural myths and stereotypes would have us believe that men are emotionally insensitive, and driven by their sexual urges alone. But the truth is that we men need intimacy, love and affection just as much as women do.

A good man is aware of this, and lives his life accordingly. He knows that an emotional and spiritual connection is more fulfilling than a one-night stand; that sex is so much more satisfying, more profound and pleasurable when you share a deep bond with your partner. His love and respect for you is more powerful than his sexual urges. He doesn't deny or repress his impulses, nor does he indulge them recklessly. He looks, appropriately and respectfully, but he does not touch.

Above all, he goes out of his way to show you that you are his priority; that he loves you, he cares for you, and out of all the beautiful women he sees every day, you are the one that he chooses, the one that he wants, that he is yours and yours alone.

Step 8

First Step To A Break Up Is Name Calling

When you're a couple with that much emotional baggage, passions definitely get inflamed during arguments and, if you're not careful, that's when people start calling each other names. And names might sound like a minor thing to worry about. If you're screaming at each other about a truly important issue, does it really matter if someone got called a "bitch" or an "asshole"?

Yes it does. It matters because it can completely derail a fight into something much less productive and much more needlessly hurtful.

People like to deny the impact of name-calling. They say, "Oh, we're both completely foul-mouthed, we talk like sailors. We always call each other names." That may be the case, but I truly believe, both on a conscious and subconscious level, that our brains keep score during our big relationship fights. And the second our brains see a name or a personal insult on the scoreboard, everything changes.

Because the second you call your partner an "asshole," the original fight stops and a new one begins. Suddenly, everything you were arguing about before has to line up behind "WHAT did just you call me?"

Yes, if you think your loved one is being an asshole during a fight, calling them an "asshole" can be ridiculously satisfying. But it does you no favors. That one word has instantly made you the bad guy in that scenario. It's like accidentally sinking the 8-ball while playing pool - you automatically lose.

Even if your partner was being awful, if you're recounting the incident to your friends later, and it comes out that you were the first one to start throwing around the "asshole" label, sympathy will not be on your side. That may seem childish, unfair, and reductive, but it's true.

However, that doesn't mean that you can't defend yourself or let someone know that you think they're being awful. The key is just avoiding those childish, derogatory names that are so much fun to say.

If your partner is truly being an asshole, don't use that word, but feel free to tell them that they're being cold, cruel, spiteful, indifferent, thoughtless, nasty, unreasonable, ignorant, or mean. There is no problem with you whipping out your verbal thesaurus and telling them, with a great variety of phrasing, how you really think they're acting.

Because, even if the adjectives make them angry and they probably will, those are just normal, human, descriptive words. Those words might wound, but they have some inherent meaning that your partner will either understand or argue against.

But, when you call someone a "bitch" or an "asshole" - especially if they're an important person in your life - you're not trying to convey anything of any meaning. You're just trying to hurt them in the clumsiest way possible, and no one is going to listen to that. They're going to shut down immediately and try to hurt you back. It may even become abuse.

So, as hard as it can be, for the good of your relationship and your own sense of moral superiority, you cannot call any names during an argument. If you actually want your fight to accomplish something, or to be about more than just insults and cruelty, it's a necessary step you have to take. Even if they are, unquestionably, being an asshole, you gain nothing by pointing it out.

Step 9

Treat Him Like The King He Is

You burn to show him just how special he is to you. While saying, "Honey, I love you so much" may do the trick, making him feel like a king can help you communicate your true emotions. Along with getting your feelings out there, treating your guy like royalty can help boost his self-esteem or pick him up when he's feeling low. This doesn't mean that you have to lower yourself to the level of his servant. Instead, go beyond the normal everyday niceties and get creative in your quest to show him that you care.

Make a point of asking about the little things. Instead of waiting until you have a reason to call your guy - such as scheduling a date or asking for a ride - dial his number just to ask about his day. A simple act shows support and caring without going overboard. This shows your man that you are thinking about him often and that you value what is going on in his life. Add a sentimental statement that lets him know he's on your mind. You'll flatter your man by telling him that you were thinking about him.

Give sweet little gifts. Look for items that clearly take who he is and what he wants into account. For example, bring him his favorite coffeehouse drink during his break from work or download a play-list of his favorite tunes.

Cook him dinner. While this brings to mind June Cleaver, you can treat your man like a king by making a dinner that caters to his wishes. For example, if you know that avocados are his favorite food, start with a guacamole appetizer, move on to chicken with avocados as a main dish and make a side that also contains them. This shows him that it is not just a meal - it is a meal specifically for him. Take him by surprise and cook a meal for no real reason other than you want to show that you care

Pay attention to him, and only him. Put your phone down, turn away from the TV, close your laptop and listen to him when he comes home at the end of the day or the two of you are on a date. Look him in the eyes when he's speaking to you, ask questions about what he's saying and smile to show your interest.

Throw him a compliment. You don't need to shower him with praise 24-7. If you know that he is feeling unsure, find something to say that will pick up his mood or give him a compliment such as, "You look so handsome in that shirt," or, "You have the most beautiful blue eyes. I just can't look away from them."

Show him affection. Give him hugs and kisses or hold his hand to show that you are his and he is yours. Avoid making it quick. Hold on and hug him for a few minutes to show that you care.

Give him a grand offering. You don't have to start every day with an over-the-top gift, but an occasional big-time gesture, along with the little everyday trinkets that you give him, shows how much you care. Make it meaningful and don't just buy the most expensive watch at the jewelry store or pick a random vacation spot. For example, if he's been talking about a golf resort that his friend recently went to, schedule a surprise weekend getaway to the destination. Above all, apply all the relationship steps already talked in this book and more.

Step 10

No King Here

Not all relationships were meant to last, and it would be preferable to know when to end a relationship. Breaking off from a relationship would mean that all your efforts in committing yourself to your lover might go to waste and your feelings invested in your partner hold meaning only in the past. However, if your relationship was not really suitable to start out with, forcing yourself to carry on with it might not be the best thing to do.

When you are deeply in love with your partner, there is a want to stay and try to work things out even though there are things going wrong. If you have the determination and the endurance, it might be worthwhile to continue your relationship and try to find solutions for it first.

There are many who do not have the determination or the endurance, and when problems arise, they might give up easily, relying on a break up to resolve all their issues. The additional problem in such a case is the couple's lack of will to try and try again. Until they actually make an attempt to solve their problems, they could not have known if they could still remain together.

Do note men who abuse their lovers. Their 'loved ones' would build up the determination to keep their relationship together, and they keep trying and trying, doing all the work and using up all their time just to be together in one place. These abusers, however, sit around and do nothing to contribute to the relationship. Relationships with these kinds of people might not be as worthwhile and you might want to end your relationship at this point.

Some relationships, such as the one mentioned earlier, could be one of those that should not be continued. There are also other types of relationships with issues that should tell you continuing the relationship would be wrong. Other relationships could be more difficult to analyse and decide on. These relationships should tell you outright that you need to leave, but when you look at your needs and wants, leaving is actually the wrong option. However, if you were to stay, the same problems will surface and start create trouble again.

One example to discuss here would be the problems of your man having an affair. When you made the decision to enter into a relationship, you made it perfectly clear that you were strictly a one guy kind of girl. You never once had a wandering eye or even played with the thought of cheating on someone, so why would you ever stick with a man who can't say the same about you? In relationships, it's super important to treat the other person the way you would want to be treated. By taking on the "boyfriend/girlfriend" title, you both are making a commitment to be with only each other. If your guy cheated on you, apparently you were the only one taking the relationship seriously, not him. You deserve the same amount of respect and appreciation that you would give to your partner when it comes to relationships, and if he's not playing by the same rules then it's time for him to get eliminated from the. The point is pretty simple: you would never cheat on him, so there is absolutely no reason to let him get away with cheating on you.

You thought you had a King you could trust and be with for years to come, but he ruined everything once he made the decision to step outside of the relationship. Getting cheated on is an excruciating experience, and anyone who makes you feel that way is not worth being with at all. The fact of the matter is simple: a man who cheats is clearly not a King (and honestly, there's a very high probability that he never will be, either. If we're talking about the long-term, just ask yourself what kind of husband that would make him while you're at it. Of course, there is just no way that you would want to be with someone who doesn't have what it takes to be someone's life partner. A guy who cheats doesn't want only you, he wants you and everyone else, and that's just not going to fly. A cheating man definitely isn't boyfriend material in your book – and the next time he cheats it will be on someone else because you absolutely aren't sticking around and waiting for him to strike again.

There are tons of things that your boyfriend can do that can be chalked up as a simple mistake and can be remedied with the words "I'm sorry" and "it won't happen again." Unfortunately for him, cheating is not one of those things. Yup… cheating on you is a completely unforgivable thing to do, and once you find about his infidelity, the damage has already long been done. If you fall for his lies, you're basically a total fool. Sure, there are definitely people out there who try to forgive and forget acts of scandalous cheating, but it's an uphill battle that's usually not worth fighting for. Once you become aware of his cheating ways, it will become nearly impossible to get the thought of him with another woman out of your head. You might find yourself becoming paranoid, overly possessive, or a total mess because of the careless choices that he made. Let's be honest – putting yourself through all of that anguish just to salvage your toxic relationship with a guy who cheats really isn't something you need, is it? Do yourself a favor and dump the cheater long before he even gets a chance to beg for your forgiveness. What's done is done, and now is the perfect time to be done with him.

Conclusion

The goal of this book was only to help. To build new families, and to bring understanding to current couples. I wanted to break this into step so, it would be easy to follow. There is nothing more beautiful than a man and a woman together. Yin and Yang together forever.

Don't miss out!

Visit the website below and you can sign up to receive emails whenever Larry Wooten publishes a new book. There's no charge and no obligation.

https://books2read.com/r/B-A-SVUI-LBPAB

BOOKS 2 READ

Connecting independent readers to independent writers.

Printed in Great Britain
by Amazon